CALL ME COLORFUL

DR. CAROL SEAY

Published by DivBooks

Dedication

To All of God's Little Children's.

You Are Precious In His Sight.

RED, YELLOW, BROWN, BLACK, and WHITE

You Are A Gift From God!

Acknowledgment

Thank You Jesus for what You have Done!

Thank You Jesus for what You are Doing!

Thank You Jesus for what You are yet going to Do!

Contents

About the Author

Dr. Carol Seay resides in Americus, Georgia, though her extensive travels have broadened her horizons. She is a devoted mother to her adult son, Ja'Marcus Ingram, and a loving sister to Corliss, Sara, Fred, and Tyrone. Known for her warm and inclusive spirit, Dr. Seay is a cherished friend to many, an inspiring teacher, and a dedicated mentor to girls aged 8 to 16. Above all, she is a servant of God, committed to making a positive impact in the lives of those around her. Dr. Seay is truly one of a kind, embracing her uniqueness with grace and purpose.

Preface

Because of the many names, I was given as a child growing up. My take on that is; to display the many colors that you would find here on planet Earth. Colors are in, out, and everywhere. If you looked up, Colors. Go ahead; and look down, beautiful Colors. Now; go round and round. Nothing but amazing, Gorgeous, Colors. Planet Earth is Nothing less but *COLORFUL!*

Introduction

I’m Free, not because I was a slave; but, because of who I am and who’s I am.

I’m Free, not because of my skin color; but, because of the color of my soul.

I’m Free, not because I’m in shacklers; but, because no more chains holding me.

I’m Free, because of the Cross at Calvary.

I’m Free, because my Creator has made me Free.

Therefore; I’m FREE indeed!

Colorful Words

C is the third letter of the English alphabet.

Canary –A small yellow songbird; a bright yellow color.

Cantaloupe –A melon with a ribbed, rough rind and orange flesh.

Carnation –A type of garden flower usually pink, red, or white.

Cherry –A small, fleshy, round fruit with a stone-like seed, usually red in color.

Chile / Chili –The very pungent pod of the red pepper

Chlorophyll –A green coloring matter in plants

Cocoa –A dark brown powder made from crushed cacao seeds, used in making chocolate. A drink made from this powder.

Color –The quality which allows one to see the difference between two things which are exactly the same shape and size: The primary colors are red, yellow, and blue. There are many other colors and many shades of each color.

Copper –A reddish-brown color.

Corn –A type of cereal crop with big, usually yellow seeds.

Cranberry –The edible, small, tart, red berry of a kind of shrub, used for making jelly and sauce.

Cream –The yellowish, fatty liquid that rises to the top of milk.

Crimson –A deep, purplish red color.

Crocus –A small plant, related to the irises, with purple, yellow, or white flowers that bloom early in the spring.

Crow –A large, shiny black bird.

Crust –A hard, usually brown outer layer of baked bread.

Cucumber –A long, green-skinned fruit related to the grounds and eaten as a vegetable.

O is the 15th letter of the English alphabet.

Ocher –A kind of fine pale yellow or red clay, used as a pigment in paints. The color of Ocher is dark yellow.

Olive –The evergreen tree that bears this fruit is olive green.

Olive oil –A yellowish oil pressed from olives, used in cooking, in salad dressings and in making soap.

Opposite –Differing as much as possible: Red and green are opposite colors.

Orange –A round, reddish, yellow, citrus fruit with a thick peel. Its value is its juice.

Orangutan –A large ape that has long arms and shaggy, reddish-brown hair.

Orchid –A light purple colored or unusually shaped flowers.

Oriole –Any of the North American songbirds of which the male has bright yellow or orange and black plumage.

Otter –An animal that has thick dark brown fur and webbed feet, living in or near the water.

L is the 12th letter of the English alphabet.

Lactic acid –A yellowish or clear syrupy liquid

Larkspur –A plant with tall stalks and clusters of pink, blue, or white flowers.

Lavender –A plant with small, sweet –smelling pale purple flowers, a pale bluish purple.

Lead –A black substance (a kind of carbon) used in pencils.

Leaf –A usually flat and green outgrowth of a plant stem.

Lemon –A yellow citrus fruit.

Leopard –A large, fierce, cat-like animal, yellowish with black spots, found in Africa and Southern Asia.

Lettuce –A garden plant with large, pale green leaves, used in salads and on some sandwiches.

Licorice –The black substance obtained from this root, used in medicine and candy.

Lignite –A soft, brownish – black coal.

Lilac –A shrub with clusters of fragrant purplish or white flowers.

Lima beans –A plant cultivated for its flat, edible, pale green seeds.

Lime –A small lemon-shaped, greenish – yellow citrus fruit.

Linden –A shade tree with heart-shaped leaves and clustered yellow flowers line.

Linseed oil –A yellowish oil pressed from linseed, used in making paints, printing inks, and linoleum.

Lip-stick –A stick of coloring for the lips, usually a shade of red or pink.

Litmus –A blue coloring matter that turns red in an acid solution and back to blue in an alkali solution.

Livid –Bluish gray in color.

Loganberry –A plant that is a cross between a red raspberry and a blackberry.

CALL ME COLORFUL

R is the 18th letter of the English alphabet.

Radish –A small vegetable with a red or white root which is eaten raw, usually in salads.

Rainbow –An arch of many colors that sometimes forms in the sky after rain.

Rash –Redness or small red spots on the skin.

Raspberry –A soft sweet red berry which grows on a bush.

Raven –A large black bird of the crow family.

Red –Is the color of fresh blood. Of hair, a reddish-brown color.

Resin –A yellowish or brownish sticky substance that oozes from pine trees.

Rhubarb –A plant that has thick reddish leafstalks, eaten in pies or as stewed fruit.

Robin –A common North American bird with a grayish-black back and a dull-red beard.

Rose –A sweet-smelling, flower, of various colors, with thorns on its stem. Colors: between deep pink and purplish red.

Rouge –A red cosmetic for coloring the cheeks.

Ruddy –Having a healthy pink or reddish color.

Russet –Reddish brown

F is the sixth letter of the English alphabet.

Fuchsia –A plant of the evening, primrose family with drooping flowers, usually red or pink.

U is the 21th letter of the English alphabet.

Ultramarine –A very bright, deep blue color.

Umber –A mineral used as a brown or reddish brown pigment.

Colors are so beautiful, and I'm not the only one that feels this way.

THE RAINBOW

A rainbow in the blue sky is a most beautiful sight. Have you ever thought; how did this beauty get there?

In the book of Genesis, this is the covenant that God made with Noah. After the flood that destroyed everything, except a family of eight and the animals. God told Noah; that water would not destroy the earth ever again. Therefore, the rainbow would be the covenant between God and Noah, and all generations to come.

Since the beginning of human history, rainbows have been symbols of hope to cultures across the globe.

The Rainbow is made up of many colors. They are: Red, Orange, Yellow, Green, Indigo, Blue, and Violet. These are seven visible colors at all times.

The rainbow will always represent joy and happiness.

Rainbows are more than just beautiful objects: they have meaning and significance that transcends time.

Colors of the Rainbow

We commonly identify seven colors in the rainbow: Red, Orange, Yellow, Blue, Green, Indigo, and Violet, and these seven colors; have come to represent feelings and emotions.

Red represents passion and vitality. Orange represents endurance and perseverance. Yellow represents happiness and cheer. Green represents growth and renewal. Blue represents calmness and serenity. Indigo (deep blue) represents awareness and intuition. Violet (purple) represents imagination and creativity.

What a beautiful sight to behold after the rain!

What is a rainbow, and why the first color in a rainbow is Red and not blue?

A rainbow is an atmosphere phenomenon; which is caused by reflection, refraction, and dispersion of sunlight from condensed water droplets resulting in a "spectrum of light" (a band of colors) appearing in the sky, that takes the shape of a multicolored arc.

Due to dispersion, white light (sunlight) separates into different components of light by their different degrees of refraction according to wavelength.

It separates into a total of seven different colors, and the band of colors starts with red on the outside and changes through orange, yellow, green, blue, indigo, to violet on the inside.

In the visible spectrum, colors follow the order of their frequencies and the wavelengths.

Red has the highest wavelength and least frequency, while violet has the least wavelength and highest frequency.

It means that red is the least refracted wave (least scattered wave) while violet is the most refracted wave (most scattered wave).

Violet has the highest energy among visible light and red has the lowest. When sunlight hits drops of water, it is refracted in a cone-like manner, with the highest frequency light at the center and fading to lower frequencies at the edges. Violet has the highest energy among visible light and red the lowest.

When sunlight hits drops of water, it is refracted in a cone-like manner, with the highest frequency light at the center and fading to lower frequency at the edges.

Hence, the start of the rainbow color is the least refracted, then, gradually changing up to the most refracted (violet). The order always remains the same because as the wavelengths going from longest to shortest, so we see the corresponding colors in this order: red, orange, yellow, green, blue, indigo and violet.

What colors are the planets in our solar system? The planets in our solar system are a veritable rainbow of colors.

What is the exact color of Earth? Earth is mostly blue, with some green, brown, and white. There are several main colors of the planet Earth, the dominant color being blue. This comes from the oceans and the atmosphere.

And above the firmament that was over their heads was the likeness of a throne, as the appearance of a sapphire stone: and upon the likeness of the throne was the likeness as the appearance of a man above upon it.

And I saw as the color of amber, as the appearance of fire round about within it, from the appearance of his loins even upward, and from the appearance of his loins even downward, I saw as it were the appearance of fire, and it had brightness round about.

As the appearance of the bow; that is in the cloud in the day of rain, so was the appearance of the brightness round about.

This was the appearance of the likeness of the glory of the LORD. And when I saw it, I fell upon my face, and I heard a voice of one that spake (Ezekiel 1:26-28). KJV

This figure "like that of a man" revealed God's holiness and prepared Ezekiel for what God was about to tell him. The figure represented God himself on the throne. In a similar way, Christ revealed God in human form and prepared us for his message of salvation. Christ came into history in a real, human body.

The glory of the Lord appeared like fire and a glowing halo or rainbow to Ezekiel. Ezekiel fell face down, over-whelmed by the contrast between God's holiness and his own sinfulness and insignificance.

Eventually every person will fall before God, either out of reverence and awe for his mercy or out of fear or his judgment. Based on the way you are living today, how will you respond to God's holiness?

The four living beings and the four wheels are powerful pictures of judgment, yet the rainbow over the throne symbolizes God's never-ending faithfulness to his people. Just as God sent a rainbow to Noah to symbolize his promise never again to destroy the earth by a flood (Genesis 9:8-17), so this rainbow symbolizes God's promise to preserve those who remain faithful to him. The purpose of God's judgment is to correct us and, ultimately, to allow perfect peace and righteousness to reign on the earth forever.

And he that sat was to look upon like jasper and a sardine stone: and there was a rainbow round about the throne, in sight like unto an emerald (Rev. 4:3). KJV

The jasper stone was a clear stone—probably a diamond—and speaks of light. Because God is light, He's not in the dark about your disappointing marriage, your distressing physical affliction, or your depressing financial situation.

The sardine stone was most likely a ruby, which of course, is red. Truly, the ruby-red blood of Christ flowed from His veins as the nails pierced His hands, as the crown of thorns was clubbed into His skull, as the spear sliced into His side.

And through it all, He would declare, “There’s nothing more I could ever do or say to prove to you I am in love with you.”

In Exodus 28, we read that the high priest wore a breastplate upon which were twelve stones—one for each tribe. The first of the twelve sons of Jacob was Reuben. Reuben’s name means “behold” or “see, a son.” His stone was the sardine stone. The last of the twelve sons was Benjamin, whose name means “son of my right hand.” Benjamin’s stone was jasper. Thus, this One on the throne is, "Behold, the Son of My right hand." It's Jesus.

The throne of God is not surrounded by danger signs or warning lights. It's surrounded by a rainbow emblematic of grace. That is why we are not instructed to come boldly unto the throne of service, intense worship, or clean living. We are invited to come boldly unto the throne of grace.

CALL ME COLORFUL

AARON'S ROBE

The robe of Aaron, the high priest of Israel, holds significant symbolism and importance in the Bible. Described in Exodus 28: 31-35; the robe was an integral part of the priestly garments worn by Aaron when he ministered before the Lord in the tabernacle. The robe was made of blue fabric, with pomegranates and golden bells alternating along the hem. These symbols were not merely decorative but held deeper meanings and served specific purposes.

The color blue in the robe symbolized heavenly origin and the divine nature of the priestly office. Blue was a rare and expensive dye in ancient times, signifying the uniqueness and sacredness of the priesthood. It reminded the priests of their heavenly calling and their role as mediators between God and the people.

The pomegranates on the robe represented fruitfulness, abundance, and fertility. The pomegranate was a symbol of prosperity and blessing in the ancient Near East. By adorning the hem of his robe with pomegranates, Aaron symbolically carried the blessings of God with him as he performed his priestly duties.

The golden bells attached to the pomegranates served a practical purpose during Aaron’s ministry. As he moved within the tabernacle, the sound of the bells would signal his presence to the people outside. The tinkling of the bells was a reminder of the priest’s intercessory role on behalf of the people and his constant connection with God.

The robe of Aaron, with its intricate design and symbolic elements, emphasized the holiness and sanctity of the priesthood. It set Aaron apart as the high priest of Israel, called to represent the people before God and to intercede on their behalf. The robe served as a visual reminder of the priest’s sacred duties and his unique relationship with God.

In Christian theology, the robe of Aaron is often seen as a foreshadowing of the role of Jesus Christ as the ultimate high priest. Jesus, who offered himself as a sacrifice for the sins of humanity, is depicted as the eternal high priest in the order of Melchizedek. Like Aaron, Jesus intercedes on behalf of believers before God, bridging the gap between humanity and divinity.

Overall, the robe of Aaron in the Bible carries rich symbolism and profound significance, reminding believers of the sacredness of the priesthood, the blessings of God, and the intercessory role of the high priest. It serves as a powerful reminder of God's presence among His people and His desire for a close relationship with them.

Aaron's robe was described as "the robe of the ephod, all of blue" in the biblical text.

THE EPHOD

The ephod was made for Aaron as a sacred garment worn by the high priest of Israel. It was a symbol of his authority and role as the mediator between God and the people. The ephod was made of fine linen and embroidered with gold, blue, purple, and scarlet threads. It also had two shoulder pieces with onyx stones engraved with the names of the twelve tribes of Israel, symbolizing Aaron's role in representing the entire nation before God. The ephod was an important part of the high priest's attire and was worn during rituals and ceremonies in the Tabernacle.

The ephod was an apron which extended to the knees—a most fitting garment for one involved in the work of preparing animals for sacrifice. The ephod speaks of Christ, the Authoritative One, because in Old Testament culture, the ephod spoke of authority. After Gideon led the people of Israel to victory over their enemies, the Midianites, the people asked him to be their king. Gideon refused, saying it was the Lord who would rule them.

BREASTPLATE

Breastplate is an ornament covering the breast of the high priest, first mentioned in Exodus 25:7. It was made of embroidered cloth, set with four rows of precious stones, three in each row.

Worn over the ephod (a priestly garment), the breastplate was a significant piece representing divine judgment and revelations. The high priest's breastplate, referred to as the "Breastplate of Judgment" or "Breastplate of the Urim and Thummim," underpins the concept of divine guidance and revelation in the scriptures.

Described in Exodus is the Breastplate of Aaron, a sacred object worn by the High Priest of the Israelites in order to communicate with God. Worn over the Priest's sacred vestments, it was attached by shoulder straps at the corner and contained twelve gemstones.

The breastplate with 12 stones mentioned in the Bible holds significant meaning and symbolism, representing the divine connection between God and the high priest. According to the Book of Exodus, God instructed the high priest to wear a breastplate made of 12 different gemstones while praying. The stones represent the complete family of God and symbolize God's loving leadership.

Each stone is engraved with the names of the 12 tribes of Israel. The breastplate also included mystical objects called Urim and Thummim, which were used for divine guidance. The placement of the stones on the breastplate follows the birth order of Jacob's sons, starting from the far right. The purpose of the breastplate was to remind the high priest of his role as a mediator and intercessor for the people. It also served as a memorial before God and a reminder of the priest's obligations to both God and the people. Seeing the tribes represented on the breastplate helped the people feel seen, remembered, and cared for by God.

Tribes	**Stones**
Reuben	Sardius (Ruby)
Simeon	Topaz
Levi	Carbuncle (Garnet)
Judah	Emerald
Dan	Sapphire
Naphtali	Diamond
Gad	Ligure (Jacinth)
Asher	Agate
Issachar	Amethyst
Zebulun	Beryl
Joseph	Onyx
Benjamin	Jasper

By wearing the breastplate with the stones in their designated order, the high priest carried with him the representation of God's divine plan for the people of Israel. It served as a constant reminder of the chosen nature of each tribe and their collective responsibility to fulfill their God-given purpose.

As the high priest wore the breastplate, he carried the weight of the entire nation on his chest, symbolizing his responsibility to represent the people before God. The breastplate served as a constant reminder of the priest's role in seeking divine guidance and judgment on behalf of the people.

The high priest would bring the needs, concerns, and prayers of the people before God, seeking His guidance and intervention. The breastplate, with its engraved names and mystical Urim and Thummim, provided a tangible connection to the divine and a means of seeking God's guidance.

The breastplate was like a living tapestry, telling the story of God's faithfulness to His people. It served as a powerful and tangible symbol of His love, guidance, and protection. Seeing their tribes represented on the breastplate brought comfort and reassurance to the people.

COLORFUL STONES

The stone name: Sardius, this gemstone is Red. The Hebrew word for Sardius is oden which literally means red stone. This gem is frequently found in tombs of ancient royals.

The stone name: Topaz, this gemstone is Yellow. The name Topaz comes from Topazios, the old Greek name for a small island in the Red Sea, now called Zabargad.

The ancient Greeks believed that that topaz gave them strength.

The stone name: Emerald, this gemstone is Green. Emerald gemstones were mined in Egypt as early as 330 BC, but some estimate that the oldest emeralds are 2.97 billion years old. Cleopatra is perhaps the most famous historical figure to cherish emerald gemstones. She even claimed ownership of all emerald mines in Egypt during her reign. The Egyptians used emeralds both in jewelry and in their elaborate burials, often burying emerald stones with monarchs as symbols of protection.

The stone name: Amethyst, this gemstone is Purple. The color purple is associated with royalty, nobility, luxury, power, ambition. Think of those kings and nobles wrapped in long purple robes and the religious leaders and buildings draped in purple decorations on their most holy occasions. If it is not purple; it is not amethyst.

The stone name: Sapphire, this gemstone is a saturated shade of Blue. The word Sapphire comes from Hebrew and means "the most beautiful." It's color ranges from sky blue to transparent.

The stone name: Diamond, this gemstone is a chemically pure and structurally perfect diamond is perfectly transparent with no hue, or color. However, in reality almost no gem-sized natural diamonds are absolutely perfect. The rarest diamond color is the precious red diamond stone.

The stone name: Jacinth, this gemstone is Orange-Red.

The name Jacinth has its roots in the Greek language and is derived from the word hykinthos, which translates to the Hyacinth flower. One of the valuable stones that were placed into the Hoshen (the breastplate that was worn by the High Priest of Israel) was called Leshem in Hebrew.

The stone name: Agate, this gemstone is Colorful. Agate is a translucent variety of chalcedomy made up almost entirely of silicon dioxide. Agate is often black, white or gray but can also be exceptionally colorful. Crystals in agate are colorless in their purest form but turn red or brown with the presence of iron. With manganese, the crystals turn pink, and with chromium, a shade of green.

The stone name: Azurite, this gemstone is soft Deep-Blue. It is best known for its characteristic deep blue to violet-blue color. The blue color, known as "azure," is like the deep blue evening skies often seen above deserts and winter landscapes. Azurite is not a common or abundant mineral, but it is beautiful and its blue color attracts attention. It has been used by people in many parts of the world for thousands of years.

The stone name: Onyx, this gemstone is Colorful. People chasing to design something royal and elegant are chasing Onyx Marble Stone. Colors are Onyx Stone are: White, Black, Blue, Brown, and Red.

Onyx can be found in various regions of the world, including Greece, Yemen, Uruguay, Argentina, Australia, Brazil, Canada, China, Czech Republic, Germany, Pakistan, India, Indonesia, Madaqascar, Latin America, the UK, and various states in the United States. Onyx is mentioned in the Bible many times.

The stone name: Jasper, this gemstone is Green. In the Bible, Jasper is a gemstone that symbolizes God's purity, perfection, and glory. It's also associated with the New Jerusalem.

The stone name: Chrysolite, this gemstone is pictured as Green.

GEMSTONES OF REVELATION

In Revelation, chapter 21; there are 12 gemstones listed that are believed to be the same gemstones from the Mountain of God.

These are the 12 sacred gemstones of Revelation: Jasper, Sapphire, Chalcedony, Emerald, Sardonyx, Sardius, Chrysolite, Beryl, Topaz, Chrysoprasus, Jacinth, and Amethyst.

JASPER

Jasper is present in the breastplate and The New Jerusalem wall itself was made of jasper. It is opaque, comes in most colors, and gives courage and wisdom.

SAPPHIRE

Sapphire is found in the breastplate, wall foundations, and king's treasure. It represents the Dan tribe. It is a beautiful blue color and promotes constancy, truth, and virtue. The ancients gave the name "sapphire" also to lapis-lazuli which is also a blue stone often speckled with shining pyrites that look like they are sprinkled with gold. Sapphire is too hard to engrave whereas lapis lazuli is much softer.

AGATE

Agate was the second stone in the third row of the breastplate. The stone was associated with health, longevity, and wealth. Agate was considered to have medicinal powers in the Middle Ages, supposedly countering poisons, contagious diseases, and fever. Agate comes in various bright colors. Red agate was meant to improve eyesight.

EMERALD

Emerald is in the breastplate, the wall foundations, and the Tyre treasures.

It glitters and is a brilliant green. Emerald is actually a green beryl.

It was thought to preserve or restore sight.

It signifies immortality and incorruptibility.

ONYX

Onyx appears in the breastplate and it relates to marital happiness. Its color is white and black and sometimes includes brown.

RUBY

Ruby was a stone in the foundations of the wall. Ruby has a hardness of 9 on the Mohs scale and would have been impossible to engrave. It is translated as either a sardius or a carnelian stone in the six other versions of Scripture. Rubies are also mentioned in other places in God's word.

Like all reddish gemstones that resembled the color of blood, this gemstone was thought to make the wearer invincible to wounds.

BERYL

Beryl is in the breastplate and the wall foundations. It can be pale blue to yellowy green, although it can also be white or rose. It relates to happiness and everlasting youth.

TOPAZ

Topaz also features in all three of the important biblical references to precious stones. It signifies friendship and happiness.

TURQUOISE

Turquoise, carnelian, and lapis lazuli were the most used gems by the ancients. There are more legends associated with turquoise than with any other gemstone.

Turquoise was believed to prevent accidents, and to cure diseases of the head and the heart. It was also believed to make one invulnerable and it was placed on body armor, turbans, swords, and knives.

JACINTH

Jacinth is a breastplate and a foundation stone. It is reddish-orange in color and was thought to give second sight.

AMETHYST

Amethyst appears in the breastplate, the wall foundations, and among the king's treasures. This stone was thought to prevent intoxication. Drinkers would wear an amulet of amethyst for this reason. It is supposed to provide deep and pure love. It is a brilliant purple, close to the color of red wine.

BEAUTY

What is beauty? Beauty is qualities that are pleasing to the senses or that satisfy the mind or spirit.

Which color represents beauty?

Beauty is not defined by any particular color. Everyone is unique and beautiful in their own way.

The color that often represents beauty can vary significantly across cultures and contexts.
However, some commons associations include: Red, Pink, Gold, White, and Blue.

Red; often symbolizes passion, love, and desire. It is frequently associated with beauty in fashion and art.

Pink; represents softness, romance, and femininity often linked to beauty ideals.

Gold; conveys luxury, elegance, and richness, often seen as beautiful in jewelry and design.

White; symbolizes purity and innocence, often associated with beauty in weddings and bridal attire.

Blue; seen as calming and serene, it can represent beauty in nature; such as the sky.

He hath made everything beautiful in his time: also he hath set the world in their heart, so that no man can find out the work that God maketh from the beginning to the end (Ecclesiastes 3:11).KJV

What is meant by the beauty of the Lord? How can we explain this characteristic of God?

In what sense are we to understand Him as beautiful?

The beauty of the Lord can be defined as God possessing everything in His character that is desirable. Everything that is good and righteous has its ultimate fulfillment in the God of the Bible.

What is inside of each of us is where the real beauty resides. The beauty of the Lord should be reflected in those who believe in Jesus Christ. The good news is that we can reflect His beauty by the power of the Holy Spirit who resides inside each of us.

One of the descriptions of God's character is that of beauty. The beauty of the Lord means that, in His nature, the Lord possesses everything that is desirable. His character is one of perfection. Indeed, the Scripture emphasizes that the Lord is perfect in His beauty, His character.

COLORFUL WORLD

Hey, do you know? Stop now, do I know what? Where did all the beautiful Colors come from?

Color occupies a unique place in the average person's worldview. On one hand, color is intrinsically subjective. We all experience different emotions when we look at various colors. But on the other hand, color is inherently tied to physic and mathematics. Every color occupies a specific numerical wavelength.

We also have a third, less commonly noted, method to define color which sits somewhere between the other two. We can also define color through the lens of history. As we explore different colors we'll discover that they're tightly bound into human history.

How we define color. Before we examine specific examples, we should first take a moment to consider how language impacts our view of color. Pause for a second; to think about your favorite color. There's probably something about it which just speaks to your soul. But now think about similar colors. Can you imagine not being able to differentiate between those colors and your favorite?

For example, imagine someone who loves the color blue. He'd find it hard to imagine a world where he couldn't recognize it. But; think about how the open waters sometimes have either a blue or green tint. The two colors are extremely similar in many ways. If you only saw blue on rare occasions; you might just consider it to be a specific shade of green. And in fact; we know this happens, thanks to a tribe which has no word for blue.

The tribe simply sees blue as a variation of green. Place the color blue next to shades of green and they'd have a hard time spotting it; as the item which stands out from the rest. This specific example; has highlights that our ability to work with color is often shaped by language and cultural tradition. If people don't talk about a color; then; we'll often, simply, see it as a variant of something similar.

HISTORY of COLORS and ORIGIN

Let's take a look back in time and find out when and where each color was discovered.

Blue

Blue is one of the most well documented colors in history. We can debate which cultures were the first to work with a wide variety of different colors, however; we can be quite certain which culture identified and worked with the color blue for the first time. This also highlights why we need to consider the relationship between language, culture, and history when talking about color.

Our concept of blue; was created about 6,000 years ago in ancient Egypt. If you look at the works of ancient colors; you'll notice a similar quirk in most of them. Almost; no ancient culture talks about the color blue.

The cultures; of the ancient world, simply saw blue, as a variation on other colors. The main reason for the lack of distinction is probably due to how little chance they'd have to see examples of blue in their daily life. Blue simply doesn't occur very often in the natural world when compared to other colors.

Of course we have the sky. But it's a single example among millions of other sights in our average day.

However, ancient Egypt had the means to produce blue dye by mining a semi-precious stone called Lapis Lazuli. This means that they also had the ability to fill their world with the color blue. They could dye statues, clothing, and even their faces with blue pigment. This also means that their culture needed to develop ways to talk about variations within this pigment. It's here that we really see the birth of humanity's concept of blue as a singular color.

If you're like many, you love the many shades of blue.

You can't get enough of it in your life, and you enjoy combining any shades of blues in your decorating, in your wardrobe, and even other products you choose to buy, such as your car. You know blue makes you feel good. You know it speaks to you, and you know it often serves as one of the loveliest neutrals you get your hands on.

Do you know, blue jeans go with anything? A pop of blue in the form of a throw pillow can work on almost any couch, and when you add a piece of art that contains shades of blue to your space, it often doesn't matter what your color theme is. Space without blue just isn't complete.

Green

We know that green was used in clothing as far back as ancient Mesopotamia. This period stretches 10,000 years into the past. Ancient Mesopotamia is widely considered to be the foundation of human civilization. And the ancient Mesopotamia most certainly appreciated the color green.

We even see their appreciation of the color immortalized is surviving ceramics. This artwork shows people adorned in a variety of green costumes. We also see green used in the artwork of ancient Egypt, Greece and Rome.

A color that's as old as the trees, green has been mesmerizing Humans foe eons. Fittingly, the word green is closely related to the word "growan" which means "to grow" in Old English. Green is the color we associate with growth, vegetation, renewal and life. While it has typically been associated with nature throughout history, the color green has also held the spotlight for having special significance in various kingdom, empires, religions and societies.

While you might expect the color that gives the jungle its lushly colored canopies to be a little wild, the history of green comes with some unexpected surprises.

According to some historians, the color green is actually responsible for the death of Napoleon Bonaparte.

What's more, killing an emperor isn't even the most exciting secret there is to know about green. Take a look at the tangled, untamed history of the color green.

To understand the history of green, one must understand how green is made. Green is only a primary color of light, not when we are talking about colored pigments. The only way to create green from scratch is to mix blue and yellow.

In ancient times, Egyptians used green pigments derived from natural minerals like malachite. The Egyptians strongly associated green with rebirth and regeneration. However, preserving green pigment proved difficult for the Egyptians because most of their green hues eventually turned black after being applied to the walls of caves. For the Romans and Greeks, there was the invention of an artificial pigment with a blue-green shade called verdigris that was created using corroded copper. Verdigris was used abundantly on coins and mosaics throughout the ancient world. Even medieval monks sprinkled in some verdigris to color their sacred manuscripts.

Once chemists discovered how to engineer colors during the 18th century, the world was soon introduced to luxurious hues ranging from emerald to viridian.

While green is abundant in nature, trying to recreate this pigment for use on canvas has been quite a task throughout history. In fact, green is commonly known as the "poisonous pigment" due to the fact that the difficulty of producing this color inorganically led to some very dire situations.

A chemist from Sweden named Wilhelm Scheele concocted a bright hue of green in 1775 that turned out to be downright deadly.

At first, the color that was known as Scheele's green was a popular replacement for the lackluster mineral-based and vegetable-based dyes that came before it. It was so popular that it was used on paintings, fabrics and toys for children.

However, what people didn't realize was that a toxic compound called arsenic (the most toxic form of arsenic) that Scheele used to attain his vivid green hue was deadly.

People first began to suspect that this particular hue of green was concealing a nefarious secret; when there was a phenomenon of women in green dresses becoming sick. Next, people started to notice that children in green rooms began to fall ill. It turns out that toxic vapors from green-dyed items were causing serious health problems. In fact, it's even believed today that Napoleon Bonaparte ultimately died as a result of the toxic green wallpaper in his bedroom.

Throughout time, green has taken on many meanings. People today, can appreciate the very fluid nature of green, just by taking a moment to think of the things we associate this color with. In some cases, green is associated with health, harmony, nature and growth. However, we also associate green with sickness by describing someone's face as "turning green" when they are sick to their stomach. Someone who is jealous is also described as being "green with envy." Green is even a color of Christmas. Green is also a color closely associated with specific places. Everyone knows Ireland as the "Emerald

Isle" due to its abundant green landscape. Green is also associated with the idea of good luck when placed in the context of a four-leaf clover.

Red

An argument can be made that red is the oldest color in human history. In fact, we have evidence of it in the period of time which predates written history. Our earliest examples of the color red come from cave paintings which date back to 16,500 B.C.

The prehistoric artists created their paintings from ground red ochre. It's not just a common color from that time either.

Red was one of the only colors used in the Paleolithic era. This is due to the fact that red ochre was easily created from natural resources.

Egypt is also notable for their love of red ochre. Men and women alike would often use lipstick made of the substance. However, Cleopatra took it to the next level.

She was well known for her use of expensive blue dyes as a form of makeup. But she also had her own unique type of lipstick made from a wide variety of different substances. However, even she used a little red ochre within it for color.

Different colors have a way of evoking different emotions in people. One of the most powerful colors is red. Few would argue that the color red is capable of stirring a wide range of emotions, not to mention getting people's attention. However, one might be surprised to learn about the history of the color itself. It goes back much further than most people would ever likely believe. In virtually every culture, it has been used to convey important messages or to denote crucial cultural beliefs.

Leaders all over the world have traditionally worn the color red.

Just think about English monarchs being ceremonially placed into their respective offices while clad in red.

Women often wore red dresses along with hats of the same color. This was designed to convey power, authority and moral upstanding. By the same token, horses were often decorated with red garments in order to project a feeling of power or victory in battle. As such, red has long been known as a color associated with the power of victory in battle.

Red is a color that is very easy to see, even from vast distances. It also has a tendency to grab the attention of anyone who does see it. Therefore, it is not easily overlooked.

As a direct result, it became very popular for use in battle. That said, many people also chose the color because of its association with power, dignity and good moral standing.

Yellow

Use of yellow dyes, like red, dates back into prehistory. We've seen yellow used in cave painting which are at least 17,000 years old.

It's funny, how merely thinking about a particular color elicits so many emotions. The truth is, there is an interesting and sometimes checkered history involved with almost every color conceivable to the human mind.

It is time to delve deep into the history of the color yellow. By doing so, it is possible to discover more about the ways that different cultures viewed this color. It also becomes quite apparent why the color is still used in certain circumstances to this very day.

It probably won't come as any surprise that the color was actually used in prehistoric caves to denote important things about hunting, culture and life that existed on a daily basis. While this color isn't found as frequently as other colors in prehistoric caves, it is by no means absent. The question is, were the individuals who painted these caves using the color strictly for aesthetic purposes or were they trying to convey some type of meaning by choosing this particular color in the first place? Some individuals think that they used it simply because it was readily available, although there isn't a lot of proof to back up this theory. In reality, they could have very well been trying to convey something important by specifically choosing the color yellow. However, it is also possible that they could have been doing essentially the same thing that many artists do today – choosing a color that would complement the rest of their work and be aesthetically pleasing.

Orange

Today, the color orange often evokes memories of Halloween.

However, it has a history which predates that Holiday by a considerable margin.

Some of the oldest examples of orange date back, once again, to ancient Egypt.

Europeans wouldn't have known what to make of the color. Until the 16th century, Europe simply knew it as a variant of red. In fact, they simply called the shade "yellow-red." Orange wasn't recognized as a distinct color by English speakers until orange trees were imported from Asia.

Orange and black are particularly prominent as Halloween approaches. Not to mention that we often see the sun taking on a more orange hue as the fall draws ever closer. Even the leaves join in on the season as they take on brilliant shades of red and orange. It's little wonder that we've come to associate orange with that particular time of the year.

What might come as more of a surprise; is the full and rich history associated with the color orange. We're hardly the first culture to make this color the centerpiece of a holiday or season. However, to fully understand how orange hues have influenced humanity we'll need to go back to the birth of civilization.

Eventually, Egypt would meet Alexander the Great in 332 B.C. This marked a transition of one great power to another. Interestingly enough, ancient Rome; had their own slight variation on the color orange.

Alexander the Great would do more for the color orange than simply bringing two variants of it together. The hero of Rome is also said to have been responsible for the spread of citrus trees into Greece, Turkey, and North Africa. By 300 A.D. we see tiles in Istanbul portraying oranges and lemons.

The introduction of orange changed everything. By the 1670s Isaac Newton had officially codified orange in the color spectrum.

The next big turning point in orange's history would occur in 1809. This marked the creation of the first fully synthetic orange pigment – chrome orange.

Orange's biggest mark on the 20th century can be found in our Halloween traditions. The 1950s solidified Halloween into the holiday as we know it today.

And of course, bright orange pumpkins are now synonymous with the holiday.

We also use orange in many other aspects of our life. Orange is often used in safety jackets and even prison uniforms because it catches the eye. And of course, the art world continues to use orange as a perfect way to capture some of the most beautiful sights in nature. The most colorful and beautiful sunsets will often incorporate orange to amazing effect, and what representation of Fall would be complete without orange leaves?

Purple

The history of purple dates back to the Bronze Age.

We typically associate the color purple with royalty, power, and sometimes even unearthly entities. It's not always an easy feeling to put into words. What's more, we're often not even aware of the fact that we make those associations. We might feel particularly moved by a picture, painting or even a movie. It's only on later reflection that we consciously realize just how often purple is used within those works.

We often associate the most meaningful moments in our lives with specific colors. We sometimes associate specific feelings with various colors due to the actions of people hundreds or even thousands of years in the past. There are few better examples of this phenomenon than our associations with the color purple.

Think about all the colors you find appearing in your natural surroundings. The vast majority of people will go through a wide variety of colors in their minds. However, one color will usually be conspicuously absent. Purple certainly does appear in nature.

But it's quite rare in most parts of the world. However, the scarcity of natural purple dye has also made it highly sought after.

Our first records of humans using the color purple date back to prehistory. Ancient humans made a momentous discovery about 16,000 to 25,000 years ago in the region we now call France. We'll never know how they made the discovery. But we do know that they somehow determined that mixing manganese and hematite powder together would create a purple compound. They then used this substance to draw animals, and even trace their own hands, onto cave walls.

This important color would be lost to history for a long time in many areas of the world. We wouldn't really see much use of purple coloring in the West until the Bronze Age.

Do you recall the old saying about something being worth its weight in gold? We have a historical example of a substance worth more than three times its weight in gold. And that substance was purple dye.

Purple dyes would stay incredibly rare in the West for some time to come. This helps show why we associate purple with royalty and power. For hundreds of years; the only people who could afford purple adornments were those blessed with both riches and power.

Most people don't consciously understand why they find purple so impressive. But that's the interesting thing about cultural memory. We as individuals don't always need to understand where emotional connections come from. Our culture simply instills those emotions within us as the history of the world resonates within our aesthetic preferences.

Pink

Pink is one of the most eye-catching colors in the world.

It walks that fine line between colors; found in nature and those which come about solely through humanity's artistic innovation.

Bright pink, the honor of being the oldest known biologically generated color. But pink is also rare enough to catch our attention. This appreciation of pink is hardly unique to modern times either.

We now need to move to a more recent part of history – 18th century Europe. The 18th – century aristocrat Madame de Pompadour is known for many things. Her role as maitresse-en-titre to Louis XV made her both fashionable and slightly risqué. In modern terms, she'd be considered a top-tier social influencer.

As Madame de Pompad celebrity grew, so did people's appreciation of her fashion sense. She loved the color pink and was anything but shy about that fact.

Turquoise

Is it teal? No, perhaps it's aqua. Maybe it's blue-green. The argument may lean more toward green and then back toward blue.

Turquoise is a very versatile hybrid blue/green color that is flattering on almost every skin tone and hair color. It's a cool color for blondes, yet it can emanate warmth for brunettes and those with stark black hair. Even red haired beauties stand out in turquoise. This cannot be said for certain other colors such as oranges and lavenders.

History has brought us a truly amazing color through the turquoise stone. Should someone choose to debate orange whether a shade of blue or green is truly turquoise, teal, aqua, aquamarine, or even blue-green, it might be best simply to pick your battles and let it be a subjective judgment. In other words, these colors are pretty much all in the same family and that indicates you're all pretty spot-on. After all, you might need that time to argue the pronunciation of the city of Louisville.

Brown

We're surrounded by the color brown to such a ubiquitous level that we often take it for granted. After all, brown is the color of the very dirt which life is built upon. If there's life in an area; then, it's always built on a brown foundation. Even the blue oceans boast nutrient – rich brown dirt in their deepest depths.

However, things become more complicated as we look into the past. Our ancestors were much more aware of the color brown.

Let's travel back in time and see how the color brown has been used throughout history.

To find humanity's first uses of brown pigment; we need to go into our oldest known records. Must people know; that France has an amazing history, filled with artistic and cultural innovations. However, France's history goes back far - further than most people realize. Southern France actually contains one of the oldest examples of humanities artistic expression.

The region's Lascaux cave system contains paintings which were created about 200,000 years ago. We can't be entirely certain; why these ancient people created their paintings.

But, whatever the reason; we see countless examples of brown coloring in the Lascaux cave paintings. We don't just see a single shade of brown either.

Our next stop in the history of brown; will focus on an area often known as the birth place of modern civilization.

The most important point to keep in mind is; that the region is incredibly ancient and influential.

We often see brown coloring show up in artwork; due to the simple fact that it was made with brown material.

Moving on into the 2000s, we see the trend continuing. Brown is neither; unabashedly; embraced; or avoided. And hopefully, brown will also be remembered; as we continue to march with it through a history yet to be written.

Black

What makes black reign over all other colors?

Black has a wide range of associations. It can be linked with death, mourning, evil magic, and darkness, but; it can also symbolize elegance, wealth, restraint, and power. As the first pigment used by artists in prehistory and the first ink used by book printers, black played an important role in the development of art and literature. Today, there is even a black so black; that looking at it; makes it seem like you are looking at a void.

Prehistoric black

Black was one of the first colors used in art. Prehistoric artists used black charcoal and iron minerals to create a black pigment that they then used to paint on cave walls. This steer from the Lascaux Caves in France was painted more than 17,000 years ago, although it was only discovered in 1940; by an 18 year old French boy, who was exploring the nearby country side. The 2,000 pale-o-lithic drawing found in the cave represent humans, abstract symbols, and animals, like the black ox.

The Greeks paint it black

The Greeks developed a highly sophisticated technique for painting black silhouettes on clay pottery. Later, they inverted the technique to paint red figures on black backgrounds.

There "red figures" and "black figure" vases were signed by their makers, making them the first signed pieces of art in history.

Black devils

In Latin, the word for "black," ater is associated with cruelty and evil. "Atrocious" and "atrocity" are derived from this Latinate Stem. It is no surprise, then, that in medieval paintings the devil was often painted in black.

Masters of ink

The true masters of Eastern “ink wash painting” were artists who were able to use only black ink to capture the spirit of a scene. The best’s artists used the fewest amount of brushstrokes possible to evoke an atmosphere.

Black on white

The first printed book in the world, the Gutenberg Bible, featured black type on white paper because the contrast between the two colors was the easiest to read.

Little Black Dress

The birth of the Little Black Dress has been ascribed to Coco Chanel, who, in 1927, created a series of simple black suits and dresses that were photographed in American Vogue.

Easy to wear and always elegant, the Little Black Dress has become a wardrobe staple.

What does wearing black symbolize? It became associated with power and authority, as it was worn by royalty and the clergy. The rich and powerful adorned themselves in black garments to convey their status and dominance. Black was seen as a symbol of elegance and sophistication, often reserved for those in positions of high social standing.

What is the Holy color?

White, is a symbol of purity, innocence and holiness.

What is the color of love?

Red, is the color most commonly associated with love.

What is the color of peace?

Blue is the color of peace. In its purest form, blue represents peace and tranquility.

CALL ME COLORFUL

Colors and Meanings in a Rainbow

The rainbow is one of nature's most beautiful phenomena.

However, to spot a rainbow, you ought to be in the right place at the right time!

Are you curious to know what the colors of this beautiful arc actually mean?

"Somewhere over the rainbow, skies are blue, and the dreams that you dare to dream ready to come true," was definitely well said by Lyman Frank Baum. So, is there really a pot of gold at the end of a rainbow?

The most well-known origin story of the leprechaun's pot of gold at the end of the rainbow involves a couple of poor farmers in Ireland. When this husband and wife pulled their very last carrot out of their garden, they found a leprechaun dangling from the roots. Being captured, the leprechaun promised one wish in exchange for his freedom. The husband and wife could not decide on just a single wish, so they began wishing for everything (you know how we do).

Dismayed by their greed, the leprechaun told the couple they might have all they wished for and more if they could find his pot of gold hidden at the end of the rainbow. The leprechaun winked (don't miss it) and left the farmers to chase rainbows forever, looking for a fictitious fortune.

How do you spot a rainbow?

Spotting a rainbow has a simple rule – the body needs to be strategically placed; it should be with the back to the sun. Rainbows always appear when the 2 elements; rain as well as sunshine are present. As the sunlight enters the falling drops, it breaks up into its true colors. Seeing the spectrum of colors; across the blue skies, is a sight few are blessed to witness.

CALL ME COLORFUL

COLORS

RED

Red

This is the first or the top most color in a rainbow. The color red first brings to mind the idea of love. This is the color of energy and enthusiasm. Red is also the color with the longest wavelength, and it symbolizes vibrancy and security. It has always been known to signify passion as well.

ORANGE

Orange

Orange is the second color in the rainbow; from the top. The color orange is a combination of red and yellow. It may not be as fiery as red, but; symbolizes a lot of energy and wisdom. Orange is a very warm color, which although is dynamic, is more thoughtful and controlled. This color can increase the creativity and playfulness of a person, and bring about equilibrium in Life.

YELLOW

Yellow

The third color in a rainbow from the top is yellow. The color yellow is vibrant in itself, as it represents the color of the sun. This is known to be full of energy.

Yellow also means something bright and happy, and the usage of this color is known to bring about a proper clarity of thought in the mind of an individual, and also improve one's decision – making skills. Wisdom is usually associated with this color.

GREEN

Green

Green is the fourth or the middle color in a rainbow. This arc is associated with

Archangel Raphael which is used for healing. Within the rainbow, the green represents health, wealth, and love.

BLUE

Blue

Blue is the fifth colored arc of the rainbow.

This arc is associated with Archangel Michael.

Archangel Michael is the leader of all the archangels and represents spirituality. Within the rainbow, the blue represents a connection to water and the spirit world.

INDIGO

Indigo

Indigo is the sixth colored arc of the rainbow. Within the rainbow, the color indigo represents a bridge between the conscious and subconscious worlds.

VIOLET

Violet

Violet is the seventh and final colored arc of the rainbow. This arc is associated with Archangel Zadkeil which represents mercy.

Within the rainbow, the color violet is a mixture of red and blue representing the access to the imagination and Divine inspiration.

Rainbows are one of the most beautiful phenomena steeped in a deep history that spans all cultures and religions.

CALL ME COLORFUL

What Happened

Did you know? There's an Irish saying, "There's a pot of gold at the end of every rainbow." But it used to say, "You're as likely to find a pot of gold as the end of the rainbow."

Throw caution to the wind! This cautionary tale reminds us that relying on luck, magic, and greed can be a recipe for disaster. Instead of working hard and making strategic moves to build financial stability, people can be tricked into wasting their precious time and resources searching—metaphorically—for a pot of gold at the end of a rainbow.

That's because, if you go looking for its end, the rainbow vanishes.

Rainbows occur when water droplets – from rain, mist, waterfalls, even sea spray – hang in the air.

When sunlight enters the droplet, some will reflect off the back side and pass again out the front.

As sunlight passes twice through the water, the different wavelengths that make it up bend at different angles; which splits the entering white light into the spectrum of rainbow colors.

Your position, in relation to the sun and the water droplet, affects how much and which light reaches your eyes. Meaning, you determine how much rainbow you see.

If the sun is directly behind you, and low in the sky, the largest amount of light is reflected back toward you, and you'll see a strong rainbow.

If the sun is 90 degrees to your right or left, you'll see less reflected light and a weak rainbow.

If the sun is high in the sky or on the other side of the water droplets, no light reflects back to you, and you'll see no rainbow.

This also means that, as you move, the amount of rainbow you see changes.

If you travel far enough toward what appears to be its end, the rainbow, and your pot of gold, will gradually disappear.

Rainbows are spectacular natural light shows; that are customized for every viewer; because the location of your eyes is part of the equation.

CALL ME COLORFUL

Joseph Coat

Joseph's coat of many colors was a representation of God's "light of many colors." It was a depiction of God's glory found in the third heaven.

Joseph's coat of many colors symbolizes all the favor of God, all His divine grace, power and love, all the gifts and fruit of the Spirit – the whole thing.

It was a garment given to Joseph by his father Jacob.

The coat signified Joseph as being Jacob's choice, as the future head of the clan.

Jesus came to Earth, bringing the spiritual Coat of Many Colors which had been foreshadowed by the type, Joseph's coat. The healing for soul, mind, and body that Christ gave to the people is ours today, our Coat of Many Colors.

What colors dominate our Coat of Many Colors?

You will find the blood of Jesus, which is our redemption, represented by the crimson in the Coat.

Jesus is pure – Blessed are the pure in heart for they shall see God – and white represents purity. There must be white in that Coat.

The green of life is present, for Jesus brought life, life, life.

The gold, the healing virtue of Jesus Christ of Nazareth coming down like liquid fire, there must be plenty of that.

Blue is there, the beautiful purplish royal blue, representing the miracle power of God that I see again and again in the visions as God heals the people.

When Joseph lost his coat of many colors he also lost favor because his father, thinking him dead, was unable to help him any further. It will be the same for you, if you lose or fail to put on the Coat of Many Colors that Jesus purchased for you on Calvary.

The favor of God will not be yours. Joseph cried his heart out; he suffered agony of soul when he lost his coat. He endured much before he was able to wear the Coat of Many Colors that God had provided – the divine favor of God in Joseph's hour.

To wear the Coat of Many Colors, one must suffer much. Wearing the Coat requires more than the father – child relationship of this earth; God wants you to be a vessel completely yielded to His will. Jesus came to show you how to live in the divine favor of His heavenly Father, how to reach God.

The way includes fasting, praying, and living in the Word of God.

Down through the ages, however, people have found great difficulty following His way. Had Jesus said, for instance, "You can come to the Father by throwing great banquets, by praying only once – in – a – while, by reading the Bible only on Sunday," many would have enjoyed it. But it isn't that simple, to have all the divine favor of God, so you can wear His Coat of Many Colors.

CALL ME COLORFUL

QUOTATIONS

Color – Life is Color and Warmth and Light (Julian Grenfell).

I try to apply colors like words that shape poems, like notes that shape music (Joan Miro).

Obedience is the mother of success, and the wife of security (Aeschylus).

It is much safer to obey than to rule (Thomas a Kempis).

Life is as tedious as a twice – told tale, vexing the dull ear of a drowsy man (Shakespeare).

Life is just a bowl of cherries (Lew Brown).

I have nothing to offer but blood, toil, tears, and sweat (Winston Churchhill).

I'll make him an offer he can't refuse (Mario Puzo).

God is no respecter of persons (Bible).

We must never forget that the only real source of power that we as judges can tap is the respect of the people (Thurgood Marshall).

Man was born free, and everywhere he is in chains (Jean-Jacques Roussean).

Give me liberty, or give me death! (Patrick Henry)

Unity in variety is the plan of the universe (Swami Vivekananda).

How do I love thee? Let me count the ways (Elizabeth Barr Browning).

All you need is love (Lennon / McCartney).

Love means not ever having to say you're sorry (Erich Segal).

LETTERS in COLORFUL

C in Colorful is **COURAGE.**

Courage means: Bravery; ability to control fear in the face of danger, pain, etc.

O in Colorful is **OBEDIENCE.**

Obedience means: Submission to authority.

L in Colorful is **LIFE.**

Life means: Fact of existence.

O in Colorful is **OFFER.**

Offer means: Present for acceptance.

R in Colorful is **RESPECT.**

Respect means: High esteem.

F in Colorful is **FREEDOM.**

Freedom means: The state of being free, not under control.

U in Colorful is **UNITY.**

Unity means: The fact or state of being one.

L in Colorful is **LOVE.**

Love means: A strong feeling of affection and concern for a person.

CALL ME COLORFUL

GOD'S RAINBOW COLORS

Red is towards the sky denoting the Blood of Jesus. The blood you have smeared on your doorposts will serve as a sign. When I see the blood, I will pass over you. This plague of death will not touch you when I strike the land of Egypt (Exodus 12:13). NLT

Yellow. As Jesus suffered on the cross, we go through trials and afflictions, which are supposed to refine and purify us, but without Christ's help, we might not get all the benefits of the troublesome times.

Though he were a Son, yet learned he obedience by the things which he suffered; And being made perfect, he became the author of eternal salvation unto all them that obey him (Hebrews 5:8-9). KJV

Jesus' human life was not a script that he passively followed. It was a life that he chose freely. It was continuous process of making the will of God the Father his own. Jesus chose to obey, even though obedience led to suffering and death. Because Jesus obeyed perfectly, even under great trial, he can help us obey, no matter how difficult obedience seems to be.

Christ was always morally perfect. By obeying, he demonstrated his perfection to us, not to God or to himself. In the Bible, perfect usually means completeness or maturity. By sharing our experience of suffering, Christ shared our human experience completely. He is now able to offer eternal salvation to those who obey him.

Green = Life. In him was life; and the life was the light of men (John 1:4). KJV

The darkness can never extinguish it means the darkness of evil never has and never will overcome God's light. Jesus Christ is the Creator of life, and his life brings light to humankind. In his light, we see ourselves as we really are. When we follow, the true Light, we can avoid walking blindly and falling into sin. He lights the path ahead of us so we can see to live.

Blue, Points; to the Word of God Jesus, who has heaven's authority.

And Jesus came and spake unto them saying, all power is given unto me in heaven and in earth. Go ye therefore, and teach all nations, baptizing them in the name of the Father, and of the Son, and of the Holy Ghost (Matthew 28:18-19) KJV.

God gave Jesus authority over heaven and earth.

On the basis of that authority, Jesus told his disciples to make more disciples as they preached, baptized, and taught. With this same authority, Jesus still commands us to tell others the Good News and make them disciples for the kingdom.

Jesus' words affirm the reality of the Trinity. Some people accuse theologians of making up the concept of the Trinity and reading it into Scripture. As we see here, the concept comes directly from Jesus himself. He did not baptize them in the names, but in the name of the Father, Son, and Holy Spirit. The word Trinity does not occur in Scripture, but it well describes the three-in-one nature of the Father, Son, and Holy Spirit.

The disciples were to baptize people because baptism unites believers with Jesus Christ in their death to sin and their resurrection to new life.

Baptism symbolizes submission to Christ, a willingness to live God's way, and identification with God's covenant people.

Telling them to listen to the Gospel, this is important.

Indigo represents Jesus the mystery to mankind. He is Spirit; we are flesh that cannot quite understand what He is. Christ was sent by God, to us to portray the character and nature of the Holy Trinity. Nobility!

To Jesus, it was a mystery that His disciples did not know Him.

Jesus replied, "Philip, don't you ever yet know who I am, even after all the time I have been with you? Anyone who has seen me has seen the Father! So why are you asking to see him? (John 14:9) NLT

Jesus is the visible, tangible image of the invisible God. He is the complete revelation of what God is like. Jesus explained to

Philip, who wanted to see the Father, that to know Jesus is to know God. The search for God, for truth and reality, ends in Christ.

I and my Father are one (John 10:30). KJV

This is the clearest statement of Jesus' divinity he ever made. Jesus and his Father; are not the same person, but they are one in essence and nature. Thus, Jesus is not merely a good teacher – he is God. His claim to be God was unmistakable. The religious leaders wanted to kill him because their laws said that anyone claiming to be God should die. Nothing could persuade them that Jesus' claim was true.

Violet / Purple, is the color of royalty and priesthood. Jesus is our High Priest near God bringing our requests / Prayers to the All-Mighty.

There are no "saints" needed, only Jesus.

The rainbow in Ezekiel 1:28 is a symbol of God's glory and power.

All around him was a glowing halo, like a rainbow shining through the clouds. This was the way the glory of the LORD appeared to me. When I saw it, I fell face down in the dust, and I heard someone's voice speaking to me (Ezekiel 1:28). NLT

Ezekiel fell, face down, over – whelmed by the contrast between God's holiness and his own sinfulness and insignificance. Eventually, every person will fall before God, either out of reverence and awe for his mercy or out of fear of his judgment. Based on the way you are living today, how will you respond to God's holiness?

CALL ME COLORFUL

COLORFUL FLOWERS

Anthurium

Anthurium is an accent flower. It comes in green, red, blush, orange, white, red and green, and red and white.

Stock

This inexpensive filler comes in dusty peach, dusty pink, white and lavender.

Clematis

This graceful, star-shaped flower comes in a handful of colors – from purple to magenta to a striped white.

Hyacinthus

This flower is hyper-scented. It comes in pink, green, white, blue, peach, and soft yellow.

Lilac

It's highly fragrant and comes in two shades of white and mauve.

Leucocoryne

Its flowers range in color from white to pink to deep purple.

Parrot Tulip

This flower comes in a huge range of colors, from the softest pink to the brightest coral to the deepest blackened eggplant.

Anemone

This modern – looking flower comes in white, blue, red, plum, and blush.

Nerine

This quirky flower comes in white, fuchsia, and salmon.

Dendrobium Orchid

This flower come red, white, purple, green, and magenta.

Queen Protea

This statement flower comes in soft pink and white. It’s great if you love the look of a single flower in lieu of a bouquet.

Scabiosa

These flowers are pink and light pink. They also come in white, lavender, blue, burgundy, and black.

Garden Rose

A garden rose gives off a Victorian vibe and is available in every color except blue. It is also one of the more fragrant roses and is pricier than the average rose.

Mokara Orchid

This orchid variety also comes in orange, yellow, cream with pink dots, green, and lavender. It's the most budget – conscious orchid.

Quince

This flowering branch come orange, white, and blush.

Gloriosa Lily

This flower – also known as a flame – lily also comes in yellow and orange – and – yellow.

Camellia

This glossy – leafed branch blossoms in winter and spring only. It comes in red, pink, blush, and white.

Gerbera Daisy

The flirty, youthful daisy is for the playful bride on a budget. It comes in fun colors (including pastels) and is scent – free.

Ginger

This long – stemmed flower, comes in red, pink.

Croton Leaf

This leaf comes in red, orange, yellow, and green.

Chocolate Cosmos

This comes in deep red and deep burgundy. They smell like chocolate.

Sweet Pea

Sweet Peas come in magnificent colors, give off a very light fragrance, and add a lot of texture to a bouquet.

Lisianthus

This flower is white with pink, also comes in white, green, cream, mauve, lavender, purple, white with purple, and white with mauve.

Godetia

This flower adds a vibrant pop of neon pink. It also comes in soft pink, lavender, white, and salmon.

Peony

This popular wedding flower is pink and also available in white, magenta, deep red, burgundy, and soft yellow.

Cherry Blossom

A flowering branch, that comes in pink and white.

Snapdragon

This flower comes in deep burgundy, red, orange, white, yellow, pink, and lavender.

Icelandic Poppy

This paper-thin petal and curvy stem are found in shades of pink, orange, peach, yellow, cream, and white.

Oriental Lily

This flower comes in hot pink, white, and yellow.

Agapanthus

Agapanthus comes in white and blue.

Daffodil

While the bloom comes in yellow, orange, and peach, the white variety is elegant.

Chrysanthemum

This sturdy Bloom comes in white, lavender, yellow, and mauve.

Gardenia

This blossom is available in white, yellow, and pink.

Ranunculus

Ranunculus flowers are in every color except blue. It's available in a vast array of sizes and shapes.

Cymbidium

This silky bud also comes in green, cream, mauve, burgundy, and brown.

Pansy

It comes in many color combinations.

Delphinium

This flower is often used in large ceremony arrangements. It comes in purple, white, mauve, peach, and shades of blue.

Hydrangeas

This colorful flower comes in white, green, blue, purple, and assorted pinks.

Tweedia

Besides hydrangea, tweedia is the only flower that comes in sky blue also comes in white.

Muscari

Also known as grape hyacinths and it also comes in white.

Water Lily

This aquatic flower comes in white, blue, hot pink, and yellow.

CALL ME COLORFUL

WHY ARE COLORS IMPORTANT?

Why are colors important in our lives? Something we often take for granted, but plays a large role in our daily lives: colors. From the clothes we wear to the very décor in our homes, colors influence our mood, creativity, and even our decisions. Let's just throw caution to the winds and explore the wonderful world of colors.

Do you know how certain colors can quickly lift your spirits? Bright yellow and sunny oranges can evoke feelings of happiness and warmth, while calming blues and greens can help you feel more relaxed. It's no wonder that many people choose colors based on how they want to feel!

If you draw or know someone who enjoys crafting, you'll know that color is a vital part of the creative process. The right palette can spark inspiration and help bring your ideas to life. Imagine, sitting down to sketch with a selection of vibrant reds, cool blues, and earthy greens – it's just like having a conversation with your materials. Colors can always push you to think outside the box and explore new avenues.

Colors can carry cultural meanings that can vary widely across the globe. In Western cultures, white is often associated with purity and weddings, while in some Eastern cultures, it signifies mourning.

Understanding these nuances can deepen our appreciation of art, fashion, and even everyday objects. It's fascinating to see how color can bridge gaps and create connections between different cultures.

Think about your daily routines: what to wear, what to decorate with, or even what to eat. Colors, plays a huge role in all of it.

Retailers often use color psychology to influence our shopping habits. Do you pay attention how fast food places use red and yellow? Those colors are known to stimulate appetite and grab attention.

Next time you go shopping; see if you can spot how colors influence your choices.

In today's world, sometimes; it can feel a bit dull or overwhelming, so to sprue it up try adding color can be a simple way to inject joy into our lives. Whether it's a bright floral arrangement on your dining room table or a crazy piece of art on the wall, these splashes of color can brighten your day and create a positive vibe in your space.

So, next time you're feeling a bit low or uninspired, take a moment to think about the colors around you. They're more than just pretty shades; they're mood enhancers, creativity, boosters, and cultural storytellers. Embrace the vibrant hues of Life, and let them inspire you every day!

It is hard to imagine a life without color. The truth is we don't all exactly know the colors that someone else sees. We all probably see colors a little differently, different shades, different tones, and hues. We know that color blindness exists and some people cannot see colors and instead live in a world of muted colors.

Color communicates so much. It has the power to convey moods and feelings like when people say, “He was green with envy,” “I’m feeling blue” or “She was red hot, she was so mad.” Color is used to organize life and bring order, like stop lights, or yellow versus white directional stripes on the road.

Color has the power to place stresses and strains or peace and tranquility simply by their presence in your space.

Cool tones are generally associated with peaceful things. Green is usually associated with nature, trees, grass, and peaceful scenes. Blue is often associated with blue skies or glassy waters, both calming things in nature.

I love colors and I believe color is more important than we realize.

I leave you with this: How does color affect you?

CALL ME COLORFUL

COLOR'S ATTRIBUTES

Warm colors can be inviting, comforting, and stimulating, and invoke powerful feelings like joy, playfulness, and passion.

Red attributes love, passion, heat, joy, energy, and life.

Orange attributes warmth, change, and health.

Yellow attributes happiness, cheer, warmth, optimism.

Pink attributes romance, gentleness, sweetness, playfulness.

Gold attributes riches, luxury, and tradition.

Cool colors have a calming effect and will help you relieve stress and make you feel refreshed.

Blue attributes calm, wisdom, importance, trust, and integrity.

Green attributes health, growth, environment, tranquility, and harmony.

Purple attributes wealth, nobility, luxury, spiritualism, magic, creativity.

White attributes innocence, cleanliness, clarity, and openness.

Black attributes authority, power, elegance, and mystery.

Colors play a vital role in our lives and how we respond to our surroundings.

The colors you surround yourself with can influence your perspective and emotions, as well as those around you.

CALL ME COLORFUL

BIBLE COLORS

Understanding what different colors symbolize can help us gain a deeper understanding of Scripture and give us revelation in our faith walk.

There are three primary colors found in nature. They are red, yellow, and blue.

Red: Red is translated in the Old Testament as oudem, which means "red clay." It is the root word for mankind. Adam and Esau have their names derived from the word oudem.

And the LORD God formed man of the dust of the ground, and breathed into his nostrils the breath of life; and man became a living soul (Genesis 2:7). KJV

"From the dust of the ground" implies that there is nothing fancy about the chemical elements making up our bodies. The body is a lifeless shell until God brings it alive with his "breath of life." When God removes his life – giving breath, our bodies once again return to dust. Therefore, our life and worth come from God's Spirit. Many boast of their achievements and abilities as though they were the originator of their own strengths. Others feel worthless because their abilities do not stand out. In reality, our worth comes not from our achievements but from the God of the universe, who chooses to give us the mysterious and miraculous gift of life. Value life: as he does.

And the first came out red, all over like a hairy garment; and they called his name Esau (Genesis 25:25). KJV

The symbolism of red extends its meaning for mankind as a metaphor for humanity. In the Old Testament, the blood sacrifice of an animal meant atonement for one's sin.

For the life of the flesh is the blood: and I have given it to you upon the altar to made an atonement for your souls: for it is the blood that maketh an atonement for the soul (Leviticus 17:11). KJV

The above passage gives the reason for the shedding of the blood of a sacrificial animal and its meaning for atonement. The blood of the animal was identified with its life; thus the blood atoned for human sin at the prize of life. In other words, human beings did not have to give their lives for sin because the animal's live was payment in their place. This principle of substitutionary atonement by the blood of another helps us understand the importance of the blood of Christ in receiving our salvation under the new covenant. As Jesus Christ shed His blood on the cross, He substituted His life for the sinner's life. Since His life was without sin and perfect before God, His blood is of infinite worth and results in perfect salvation for all who accept and follow Him.

The Israelites also painted the blood of a Passover lamb offering in order for the angel of death to pass over their homes during the tenth and final plague of Egypt (Exodus 12:1-13).

However, red is most commonly associated with the blood of Jesus Christ that He spilled as the bond price for our Salvation on the cross at Calvary.

And having made peace through the blood of his cross, by him to reconcile all things unto himself; by him, I say, whether they be things in earth, or things in heaven (Colossians 1:20). KJV

Christ's death provided a way for all people to come to God. It cleared away the sin that keeps us from having a right relationship with our creator. This does not mean that everyone has been saved, but; that the way has been cleared for anyone; who will trust Christ to be saved. We can have peace with God and be reconciled to him by accepting Christ, who died in our place. Is there's a distance between you and the Creator, be reconciled to God. Come to him through Christ.

Blue: Blue in the Bible represents the heavens and the Word of God.

In Exodus, when Moses, his sons, and 70 elders of Israel went up to Mount Sinai to worship God, they saw God and described the pavement under His feet as being bright as the blue sky.

Following this encounter, Moses received the 10 commandments.

And they saw the God of Israel: and there was under his feet as it were a paved work of a sapphire stone, and as it were the body of heaven in his clearness (Exodus 24:10). KJV

Blue is translated in Hebrew as tekelet. It is also found in the Bible to mean purple or violet.

Silver spread into plates is brought from Tarshish, and gold from Uphaz, the work of the workman, and of the hands of the founder: blue and purple is their clothing: they are all the work of cunning men (Jeremiah 10:9). KJV

Tekelet was the color assigned for priest's clothing, in particular, their hem.

In Luke 8:40-48, the woman with the issue of blood was healed by our High Priest, Jesus Christ, when she touched the hem of His garment. Therefore, blue is also accredited with being the color of God's healing and grace.

Yellow: Yellow is referenced in the Bible by the Hebrew word charuts, which refers to the precious metal gold. Gold represents the sovereignty of God. In the Old Testament, Solomon had the Temple built and overlaid in gold, even down to the priest's utensils. At Jesus' birth, one of the gifts He received was gold. And the building of the wall of it was of jasper: and the city was pure gold, like unto clear glass (Revelation 21:18). KJV

Yellow and gold also represent the presence of God and purification through fire.

Green: Green, being the color of vegetation, symbolizes life, restoration, and new beginnings. Green is also the color of resurrection, which we experience in spring.

Amber: Amber symbolizes the glory of God, His judgment, and endurance.

And I looked, and behold, a whirlwind came out of the north, a great cloud, and a fire in folding itself, and a brightness was about it, and out of the midst thereof as the color of amber, out of the midst of the fire (Ezekiel 1:4). KJV

Purple: Purple represents royalty, majesty, and priesthood in the Bible. And the soldiers platted a crown of thorns, and put it on his head, and they put on him a purple robe (John 19:2).KJV

The soldiers went beyond their orders to whip Jesus – they also mocked his claim to royalty by placing a crown on his head and a royal robe on his shoulders.

White: White refers to holiness, light, purity, redemption, and the righteousness of Jesus Christ.

And entering into the sepulcher, they saw a young man sitting on the right side, clothed in a long white garment; and they were affrighted (Mark 16:5). KJV

Mark says that one angel met the women at the tomb, while Luke mentions two angels. These accounts are not contradictory. Each Gospel writer chase to highlight different details as he explained the same story, just as eyewitnesses to a news story, each may highlight a different aspect of that event. Mark probably emphasized only the angel who spoke. The unique emphasis of each Gospel shows that the four accounts were written independently. This should give us confidence that all four are true and reliable.

Black: Black symbolizes sin, darkness, death, and catastrophe.

But I am very angry with the other nations that enjoy peace and security. I was only a little angry with my people, but the nations punished them far beyond my intentions (Zechariah 1:15). NLT

Although the pagan nations afflicted God's people beyond his intentions, God was not powerless to stop them. God used these nations to punish his sinful people. When the nations went beyond his plans by trying to destroy Israel as a nation, he intervened.

Silver: Silver is symbolic for the Word of God, divinity, salvation, and refining.

For thou, O God; hast proved us: thou hast tried us, as silver is tried (Psalm 66:10). KJV

Scarlet: Scarlet can represent sin, but it also refers to royalty.

Come now, and let us reason together, saith the LORD: though your sins be as scarlet, they shall be as white as snow;

though they be red like crimson, they shall be as wool (Isaiah 1:18) .KJV

Crimson was the color of a deep—red permanent dye, and its deep stain was virtually impossible to remove from clothing. The bloodstained hands of the murderers are probably in view here. The stain of sin seems equally permanent, but God can remove sin's stain from our life as he promised to do for the Israelites. We don't have to go through life permanently soiled. God's Word assures us that if we are willing and obedient, Christ will forgive and remove our most indelible stains.

And I have heard of thee, that thou canst make interpretations, and dissolve doubts: now if thou canst read the writing, and make known to me the interpretation thereof, thou shalt be clothed with scarlet, and have a chain of gold about thy neck, and shalt be the third ruler in the kingdom (Daniel 5:16). KJV

Bronze: Bronze stands for strength and durability. As an alloy, it is hard and durable and was used to make the ten brazen lavers, which were basins for washing and the Molten Sea, a large basin for ablution of the priests in the temple Solomon built. In the Book of Revelation, Jesus' feet are described as been like bronze.

And his feet like unto fine brass, as if they burned in a furnace; and his voice as the sound of many waters (Revelation 1:15). KJV

His feet were as bright as bronze refined in a furnace, and his voice thundered like mighty ocean waves. (Revelation 1:15). NLV

A myriad of colors is represented in Genesis 9:13 when God sends a rainbow after the flood.

The rainbow is a symbol, for the covenant that God made with us; to never destroy mankind or any living creature again.

The point is this: God remembers His covenant, that it is everlasting. The rainbow is a sign that He remembers.

CALL ME COLORFUL

DIFFERENT SHADES of COLORS

As humanity's eyesight evolves, we may eventually see more shades of red developed and used. Red has several shades and even more variations, from pink to almost brown. Here are just some of the most used shades: burgundy, carmine, chili pepper red, cinnabar, crimson, maroon, and scarlet.

Burgundy

Burgundy is a dark red-purplish color. It takes its name from the Burgundy Wine in France. Unlike the name of the French province, you don't capitalize the "B" in the color burgundy.

Carmine

Carmine: a.k.a. Imperial, is the general term for a group of deep red colors, very slightly purplish and closer to red than crimson. Some rubies have a color called "rich carmine," while processing the raw pigment can achieve deeper and darker variations.

Chili Red

As the name implies, chili red is derived from red chili peppers. It's also the red shade used in Chile and South Africa flags.

Cinnabar

Similar to the previous entry, the color cinnabar comes from a mineral of the same name. This color has a slightly orange shade and several variations, ranging from brick red to bright scarlet.

Crimson

Crimson is an intense, deep, bright red with some hints of blue or violet making it very slightly purplish. On the RGB color wheel, crimson comes between rose and red and between magenta and red on the RYB color wheel.

RGB color system, constructs all the colors from the combination of the Red, Green and Blue colors.

RYB color system, are based on three primary colors from which all other colors in the system can be produced. The primary colors are: Red, Yellow, and Blue.

Maroon

Maroon is a brownish crimson color derived from the French word marron (chestnut).
In the RGB color model, the web color for maroon is achieved by turning down the brightness of pure red to about one-half.

Scarlet

Scarlet is a bright red color that sometimes has a tinge of orange. On the traditional color wheel, it’s a quarter of the way between red and orange and slightly less orange than vermilion.

CALL ME COLORFUL

GOD'S COLOR SPECTUM

While researching, I decided to research to see if there was a particular color that would represent God. Immediately; red came to mind. Why, because Red would represent the blood of Jesus, love, and the fire. But, shame to share; to my own surprised, I now understand that all colors represent God. They all have different significance and meanings. Believe it or not; most are very logical.

God is the foundation of the whole world and all its beauty and emotions. Knowing that colors are part of our life, each color represents all that we see and all that we feel in our hearts.

Red – Blood of Christ, Warfare, Consuming fire, Blood Covenant, Forgiveness.

Gold – Kingship, glory, His Holiness, Liberty, Authority.

Silver – Redemption, Word of God, Wisdom, God's Refining Process.

Amber – The glory and presence of God.

Purple – Is Royalty, Majesty, the Kingdom, Inheritance, Authority.

Orange – Fire of God, Harvest, Fruitfulness, Warrior.

White – Purity, Innocence, Salvation, Surrender to God, Overcomer, Holy,

Undefiled, Worthy, Honor, Righteousness.

Blue – Grace, Mercy, the River of Life, Revelation, Hope, God's Passion.

Green – Healing, Restoration, New Beginning, Prosperity, Throne Room,

Flourishing.

Pink – Faithfulness, humility, intimacy, child-like faith, First Love.

Copper/Brass

Bronze – Jesus' feet, Strength, Atonement, Forgiveness, Washing, Tabernacle

Alter, Fires of testing, offering.

Lavender – Is Standing in His Presence.

Black – Bondage, death to self, without light, judgment, sin.

Rainbow – God's promise, Radiance of God.

Genesis 1, "In the beginning when God created the universe... everything was engulfed in total darkness... Then God commanded, "Let there be light" – and light appeared. Then he separated the light from the darkness, and he named the light "Day" and the darkness "Night." Evening passed and morning came that was the first day."

From the first verse in the Bible, we see that God makes reference to light and darkness. This is the first reference to color in the Bible. He created many other colors from the blues in the sky and waters to the greens of the plants, grass, and trees. These first references to colors in nature give us the spectrum of colors as we know it today. The seven colors in the rainbow, red, orange, yellow, green, blue, indigo, and violet, represent the seven days when God created the earth.

They represent God's color spectrum. This color spectrum is the same as the color wheel that we learn about in modern day art class.

CALL ME COLORFUL

COLOR, COLOR, COLOR!

Black, blue-black, carbon, charcoal, coal, crow, ebony, India ink, ink, jet,

lampblack, pitch, raven, sable, sloe-black, soot, blue, aquamarine, azure,

blueberry, bluebonnet, cerulean, cobalt, Copen, cornflower, cyan, delft, gentian, huckleberry, indigo, lapis, lazuli, Lucerne, lupine, marine, sapphire, smalt, teal,

turquoise, ultramarine, wisteria, brown, burnt, almond, sienna, ocher, umber,

acorn, anthracene, auburn, baize, bay, beige, biscuit, brick, brindle, bronze, buff,

burgundy, butternut, camel, caramel, chestnut, chocolate, cinnamon, cocoa,

coffee, copper, doeskin, drab, dun, ecru, fallow, fawn, fox, hazel, khaki,

mahogany, manila, maple sugar, mocha, negro, nougat, nutria, ocher, pongee,

Putty, raffia, raw sienna, russet, rust, sandalwood, sepia, sienna, sorrel, tan,

tawny, toast, umber, Vandyke, walnut,
gray, flint, granite, henna, liver, merle,

moleskin, mushroom, neutral, nutmeg,
obsidian, oxblood, pelican, roan, salt and

pepper, sand, sedge, silver, slate, smoke,
taupe, wheaten, orange, apricot,

marigold, tangerine, pumpkin, grape,
lavender, lilac, coral, cranberry, hot pink,

paprika, peach, pink, poppy, ruby,
salmon, wild cherry, wine, ivory, cream,

lemon, linen, mustard, periwinkle

CALL ME COLORFUL

SUNSET COLORS

"A red sky at night is a shepherd's delight!

A red sky in the morning is a shepherd's warning."

Gaze up at the sky one evening and you're likely to see the crisp blue sky of the afternoon replaced with a reddish-orange hue stretching for miles.

You might be wondering: Why does the color of the sky change at different times of the day? The answer has to do with how light from the Sun interacts with the atmosphere surrounding the Earth.

Light travels in waves. Every color we see is determined by the length of those waves. Red wavelengths are the longest, and as you go through the rainbow the waves get shorter and shorter until you reach the blues and violets, which are the smallest.

As the Sun's light travels towards us, at first all it encounters is the emptiness of space. But here on Earth, swirling in the air around us are thousands of near-invisible particles. Dust and water droplets are the larger ones, but there are also the minuscule gas molecules—mostly oxygen and nitrogen—that make up the air itself. The wavelengths that make it to the Earth's atmosphere collide with these particles; which sends light bouncing in many different directions. Think of it like this: If you've ever been in a crowded bumper—car pavilion of an amusement park, bumping into other cars and being bumped into yourself, you've played the part of a light wave. But not all wavelengths bounce around to the same degree.

Blue wavelengths, because of their smaller size, are scattered more easily and in many directions. Red wavelengths, which are larger, are scattered the least by those tiny particles in the air.

During the day, when the light has the shortest distance to travel through the atmosphere, what we end up seeing are the blue waves that have been scattered all across the sky. At the day's end, though, the light has to travel through much more of the atmosphere, and those short, blue light waves have a tough time getting past all the molecules. They mostly get scattered away before they ever reach us. The result is that red sky we see at sunset, since longer red wavelengths are still able to penetrate the atmosphere.

So, when you see a red sky at night, just remember that it's actually the last remaining survivor of the whole rainbow of colors.

What's considered a magnificent sunset is a particularly colorful one, with hues of red, orange, and pink streaked across the evening sky. And; when it comes to color, the brighter, the better.

One last thing; affecting the likelihood of a good sunset, is clouds or lack thereof.

CALL ME COLORFUL

COLORS REPRESENT IN THE BIBLE

When it comes to colors, the Bible doesn't list every color.

Amber: Likeness of God; jewel (treasures of heaven, the word of God). "This is what the Lord looked like" (Ezekiel 1:4, 27-28).

And I looked, and, behold, a whirlwind came out of the north, a great cloud, and a fire unfolding itself, and brightness was about it, and out of the midst thereof as the color of amber, out of the midst of the fire.

And I saw as the color of amber, as the appearance of fire round about within it, from the appearance of his loins even upward, and from the appearance of his loins even downward, I saw as it were the appearance of fire, and it had brightness round about.

As the appearance of the bow that is in the cloud in the day of rain, so was the appearance of the brightness round about. This was the appearance of the likeness of the glory of the LORD. And when I saw it, I fell upon my face, and I heard a voice of one that spake.

Black: Satan; death; demonic; darkness, sin, evil, mourning; detestable. "The earth will mourn and the heavens will be draped in black" (Jeremiah 4:28). Black vulture: (Leviticus 11:13; 19:31).

For this shall the earth mourn, and the heavens above be black; because I have spoken it, I have purposed it, and will not repent, neither will I turn back from it.

And these are they which ye shall have in abomination among the fowls; they shall not be eaten, they are an abomination: the eagle, and the ossifrage, and the ospray.

Regard not them that have familiar spirits, neither seek after wizards, to be defiled by them: I am the LORD your God.

Blue: Health; royal and heavenly. God's presence, a heavenly visitation: (Numbers 4:5-7).

"Across the entrance of the Most Holy Place he hung a curtain made of fine linen, decorated with blue, purple, and scarlet thread and embroidered with figures of cherubim" (2 Chronicles 3:14).

"The blueness of a wound turns cleanses evil" (Proverbs 20:30). KJV "Feeling blue."

And when the camp setteth forward, Aaron shall come, and his sons; and they shall take down the covering vail, and cover the ark of testimony with it:

And he made the vail of blue, and purple, and crimson, and fine linen, and wrought cherubims thereon.

And shall put thereon the covering of badger's skins, and shall spread over it a cloth wholly of blue, and shall put in the staves thereof.

And upon the table of showbread they shall spread a cloth of blue, and put thereon the dishes, and the spoons, and the bowls, and covers to cover withal: and the continual bread shall be thereon:

The blueness of a wound cleanseth away evil: so, do stripes: the inward parts of the belly.

Gray: Uncertain; guessing; right vs. wrong; deception: Blind to sin and weak. "Don't think black or white." Crown of Glory: ("Gray hair is a crown of glory") (Proverbs 16:30) (Hosea 7:9).

He shutteth his eyes to devise forward things: moving his lips he bringeth evil to pass.

Strangers have devoured his strength, and he knoweth it not: yea, gray hairs are here and there upon him, yet he knoweth not.

Green: New life; garden (Garden of Eden – Tree of Life and Tree of Good and Evil (Genesis 2). Cultivate; spiritual and physical rest and renewal (Psalm 23:4 and Hosea 14:8).

Money, greed, envy, "Death I looked up and saw a horse whose color was pale green. Its rider was named Death, and his companion was the Grave" (Revelation 6:8).

Yea, though I walk through the valley of the shadow of death, I will fear no evil: for thou art with me; thy rod and thy staff they comfort me.

Ephraim shall say, what have I to do any more with idols? I have heard him, and observed him: I am like a green fir tree. From me is thy fruit found.

And I looked, and behold a pale horse: and his name that sat on him was Death, and Hell followed with him. And power was given unto them over the fourth part of the earth, to kill with sword, and with hunger, and with death, and with the beasts of the earth.

Orange: Fruit of the Spirit (something fresh and pleasant – Galatians 5:22-23). Fire (is orange). Purified; Protection ("fire by day"). "Baptize you with the Holy Spirit and Fire (Luke 3:16). God is a consuming fire. "But I tell you that anyone who is angry with a brother or sister will be subject to judgment. Again, anyone who says to a brother or sister, 'Raca,' is answerable to the court. And anyone who says, 'You fool!' will be in danger of the fire of hell" (Matthew 5:22).

But the fruit of the Spirit is love, joy, peace, longsuffering, gentleness, goodness, faith, meekness, temperance: against such there is no law.

John answered, saying unto them all, I indeed baptize you with water; but one mightier than I cometh, the latchet of whose shoes I am not worthy to unloose: he shall baptize you with the Holy Ghost and with fire:

Purple: Royalty; wealth; royal robes. Ruler: (good – Christ or evil – Pharisees). "The soldiers wove a crown of thorns and put it on his head, and they put a purple robe on him" (John 19:2; Judges 8:26).

And the weight of the golden earrings that he requested was a thousand and seven hundred shekels of gold; beside ornaments, and collars, and purple raiment that was on the Kings of Midian, and beside the chains that were about their camel's necks.

Red: Blood of Jesus; sacrifice; purifying; war; strife. Leviticus 17:11; Ephesians 1:7; Colossians 1:20; Hebrews 9:21-22 "You must not build a temple to honor my name, for you are a warrior and have shed much blood" (1Chronicle 28:3).

For the life of the flesh is in the blood: and I have given it to you upon the alter; to make an atonement: for your souls: for it is the blood that maketh an atonement for the soul.

In whom we have redemption through his blood, the forgiveness of sins, according to the riches of his grace;

And, having made peace through the blood of his cross, by him to reconcile all things unto himself; by him, I say, whether they be things in earth, or things in heaven.

Moreover he sprinkled with blood both the tabernacle, and all the vessels of the ministry.

And almost all things are by the law purged with blood; and without shedding of blood is no remission.

But God said unto me, Thou shalt not build a house for my name, because thou hast been a man of war, and hast shed blood.

White: Holiness; royalty; throne; purity; righteousness; cleansed; (Isaiah 1:18; Daniel 7:9).

Come now, and let us reason together, saith the LORD: though your sins be as scarlet, they shall be as white as snow; though they be red like crimson, they shall be as wool.

I beheld till the thrones were cast down, and the Ancient of days did sit, whose garment was white as snow, and the hair of his head like the pure wool: his throne was like the fiery flame; and his wheels as burning fire.

Yellow: Sun; seed; nourishment, Unclean. "The manna looked like small coriander seeds, and it was pale yellow like gum resin" (Leviticus 11:7; 13:30).

And the swine, though he divide the hoof, and be cloven-footed, yet he cheweth not the cud; he is unclean to you.

Then the priest shall see the plague: and, behold, if it be in sight deeper than the skin; and there be in it a yellow thin hair; then the priest shall pronounce him unclean! It is a dry scab, even a leprosy upon the head or beard.

CALL ME COLORFUL

FIRE

Have you ever wondered, what is the color of fire?

Fire is something burning with flames.

We get entranced by the flicker of the flames. We enjoy seeing the different colors they take on as they burn brightly. While the majority of the flames hover between the hues of orange and yellow, we also catch glimpses from time to time of other colors, including red, white, and blue. What causes flames to burn with different colors?

Flames take on different colors for various reasons. Two of the most important factors are temperature and the chemical composition of the fuel. First take a look at the effect temperature has on the color of flames.

Red flames correspond to temperatures from 980 F up to 1,800 F. Flames turn orange when the temperature reaches 2,000 F to 2,200 F.

When temperatures approach 2,400 F to 2,700 F, flames appear white.

The farther away from the fuel source that the flame reaches, temperature decreases, leading to the bulk of a flame often being orange while the tip is red.

There's one other color you may have seen appear in flames on a regular basis: blue.

The color blue indicates a temperature even hotter than white. Blue flames usually appear at a temperature between 2,600 F and 3,000 F.

Blue flames have more oxygen and get hotter because gases burn hotter than organic materials, such as wood.

While variances in temperature account for most of the colors visible in flames, the chemical composition of the fuel can also be a factor.

Generally, the color of a flame may be red, orange, blue, yellow, or white.

CALL ME COLORFUL

COLORS OF HEAVEN

The Bible employs brilliant colors to help describe Heaven's beauty.

The wall was built of jasper, while the city was pure gold, like clear glass. The foundations of the wall of the city were adorned with every kind of jewel.

And the foundations of the wall of the city were garnished with all manner of precious stones. The first foundation was jasper; the second, sapphire; the third, a chalcedony; the fourth, an emerald;

The fifth, sardonyx; the sixth, sardius; the seventh, chrysolite; the eighth, beryl; the ninth, a topaz; the tenth; a chrysaprasus; the eleventh, a jacinth; the twelfth, an amethyst.

And the twelve gates were twelve pearls; every several gate was of one pearl: and the street of the city was pure gold, as it were; transparent glass.

CALL ME COLORFUL

MY HAT OF MANY COLORS

My hat has Red on it. Why, because it carries so much love in it. The Bible says that God so loved the world, that he gave his only begotten Son.

Red is perhaps the most popular representation of love that is of the romantic and passionate type. This is because red is the color of blood, which symbolizes excitement, passion, and sexuality.

Red is a primary color across all models of color space. It is the color of blood. It is often associated with love, passion, and lust but also danger and aggression. It is frequently used in relation to Valentine's Day. It can also be used to signify danger or warning but it is also associated with importance. It is used for stop signs and fire engines.

Blood also runs through the heart, which is the human organ associated with feelings of love because of the increased heartbeat and racing pulses that people experience when in love.

Red is found in rainbows. It is the second most popular favorite color among humans. Red is the first pigment ever used for art.

That is why romantic love is often symbolized by a red heart.

My hat is dressed with different shades of Blue. Some of the most popular shades of blue are: dark blue, bright blue, peacock blue, turquoise, blue, and sky blue. Dark blue is a classic color that can add a touch of elegance to any space. Because blue is the color of God and his moral law. This symbolism refers to the sky, representing the sacred covenant between God and all creation.

Blue is a primary color across all models of color space. It is the color of the ocean and the sky; it often symbolizes serenity, stability, inspiration, or wisdom. It can be a calming color, and symbolize reliability. Blue can also represent sadness and depression.

My hat is embracing the color Yellow. Yellow, one of the primary colors found in rainbows, is commonly used throughout the world. Traffic lights and signs use it to symbolize caution when traveling. In most cultures, it also represents sunshine, happiness, and warmth.

Yellow is a color that represents happiness, joy, and energy. It has been linked to the Sun, which is a source of life and light.

Yellow; is a primary color in many models of color space, and a secondary in all others. It is a color often associated with sunshine or joy. It is sometimes used in association with cowardice or fear, the phrase "yellow-bellied."

Children tend to like this color, and it is used to market products to children; it is also used for warning signs, school buses and taxi cabs since it is such a bright, noticeable color.

Green represents the love that exists between people who support and nurture each other, and help each other become the best version of themselves.

Green is a primary color in many models of color space, and a secondary in all others. It is most often used to represent nature, healing, health, youth, or fertility, since it is such a dominant color in nature. It can be a very relaxing color but is also used in the US to symbolize money, greed, sickness, or jealousy.

My hat is wearing the color Green well. In Revelation, green imagery signifies new beginning and eternal life, reflecting the transformative power of Jesus Christ teachings.

In the Bible, the color green is often with life, renewal, and often associated with life, renewal, and growth.

My hat carries a pop of color. And that color is White. Why because white is associated with peace. The Bible tells us that Jesus came to give us peace.

And the peace of God, which passeth all understanding, shall keep your hearts and minds through Christ Jesus.

Thou wilt keep him in perfect peace, whose mind is stayed on thee:

White has symbolized purity, innocence, and tranquility across many cultures. When there is a surrendering; a white flag or cloth is raised and waved.

The white dove has become a universal symbol of peace.

White is a primary color across all models of color space. It most often symbolizes perfection, faith, innocence, softness, and cleanliness.

Brides often wear white dresses to symbolize purity.

My hat has Pink why because pink is a sign of hope. My hope is built on nothing less than Jesus Christ and righteousness.

The Bible says that true hope is unseen. And if we can be hopeful for one thing, such as our salvation, which is also unseen, then; we can be hopeful for other things too. It's a simple thing.

Pink is a prominent secondary or tertiary color in many color space models. It is associated with softness, sweetness, love, and immaturity.

Pink represents Compassionately Love. The compassionate and unconditional kind of is represented by the pink color. It is a soft and feminine color that adequately expresses the nurturing nature of this type of love.

Pink is a welcoming shade that gives off a feeling of warmth, comfort, and tenderness, like being wrapped in the arms of a caring friend or loved one.

Pink also signifies peace and contentment, which signifies full acceptance of one's self, faults and all.

Purple represent longsuffering.

The color of purple signifies pain, suffering, grief, and mourning and is used to acknowledge the loss of loved ones.

My hat has on it the color Purple. Why purple because it means that my head is crowned with wisdom, creativity, royalty, power, ambition, and luxury. Also it means wealth and independence. Work your thing purple.

Purple has numerous variations colors. In the Bible the Roman soldiers clothed

Jesus in purple before beating him and crucifying him.

In the rainbow of hues, Purple is the giver and do-gooder. When the world hits you hard, Purple lifts you up.

Orange is a secondary color across many models of color space. It is often associated with amusement, extroversion, fire, energy and activity.

It is the color most closely associated with autumn and leaves.

It is one of the most attention, – grabbing colors in human vision, and is often used to attract the eye (traffic cones, safety vests, etc.).

My hat is designed with the beautiful color Orange. Orange is associated with joy, creativity, and enthusiasm.

Orange symbolizes the presence of God. Orange – Fire of God, deliverance, passionate praise.

Orange is a vibrant and engaging color. It captures your attention like a never ending flame.

Black is a primary color across all models of color space. In Western culture, it is considered a negative color and usually symbolizes death, grief, or evil but also depression. People often wear black for mourning, although this practice is not as widespread as it was in the past.

Black is the strongest neutral color there is. The dark, rich, color, black; symbolizes the fertile soil from which life emerges.

The color black has long captivated the human imagination, evoking a wide range of emotions and cultural interpretations. Black was seen as a symbol of elegance and sophistication, often reserved for those in positions of high social standing.

My beautiful hat has many colors. They are: red, blue, yellow, green, white, pink, purple, orange, and black.

Why do I wear so many colors? The Bible tells us that God has no respectful of person, therefore; I have no respectful of color. They are all beautiful and welcome here. In a world of unrest, Continue to be Colorful!

Because of the colors on my hat, you are told:

“CALL ME COLORFUL”

CALL ME COLORFUL

Made in the USA
Columbia, SC
07 May 2025

57570977R00126